Leaders and those who aspire to be leaders are looking for answers.

They want them **now.**
They want them **fast.**
They want them **free.**

Purchase this book; you will get two out of three.

Copyright © 2015 by Peter Psichogios
and CSI International Publishing

All rights reserved. No part of this book may be reproduced or utilized in any form or by any means, electronic or mechanical, including photocopying, recording or by any information storage or retrieval system, without permission in writing from the Publisher. Inquiries should be addressed to CSI International Publishing, 5430 Timberlea Blvd Mississauga, ON L4W 2T7

Image Credits: Shutterstock
Hirsman, Vector, jesadaphorn, Macrovector, Arcady, faxsal, Talashow, Aleksii, McDonald, iDesign

Cover and Page Design by Patsy Psichogios

Printed in China
Preview Edition, April 2015
Published by CSI International Publishing

Psichogios, Peter
Leading From the Front Line.
How to Create Exceptional Experiences
ISBN 978-0-692-36008-8

This book is dedicated to

Madison and Thomas Psichogios, my two awesome children, on whom I have experimented my behavioral science theories. They have helped me take the BS out of the behavioral sciences.

Madison and Thomas are both well on their way to becoming great leaders!

Learn How To Create
Exceptional Experiences

LEADING FROM THE FRONT LINE

PETER PSICHOGIOS

ABOUT THE AUTHOR

Peter Psichogios is the President of CSI International Performance Group, whose mission is to help companies create exceptional employee and customer experiences. Prior to joining CSI International, Peter served as an executive member of one of the largest Instructional System Association companies in the world. In this capacity, he traveled the world developing leaders with Dr. Ken Blanchard for 15 years.

Since then, Peter has been fortunate to work with the who's who of the Fortune 500. He helps these organizations create the type of interactions that all human beings crave: Personalized, Friendly and Authentic.

INTRODUCTION

This book and these principles are appropriate for all types of leaders and anyone who aspires to be a leader. Today, organizations are faced with a new challenge of leading and developing "part-time" talent.

This book will remind you and teach you simple, but powerful, proven principles.

- Front-line leaders have the opportunity to see, learn and know more about the customer than any other type of leader in the organization.

- All people want to excel; They want skills that make them more marketable.

- Every world class leader listens to and acts on the truth!

- Internal service cooperation is paramount today.

- When you deliver skills that increase the competency of your workers, they always become more energized and engaged.

- The key to intense employee engagement is to create a culture where leaders are held accountable for developing and enabling others.

- Repetition is the mother of all learning. Repetition is the mother of all learning.

- Fast, fun and hassle free experiences rule!

- What motivates you is different than what motivates me.

- Your word-of-mouth reputation is everything.

> **Remember,
> these principles will only be
> as powerful as your committed follow up
> and reinforcement to them.**

LEADING FROM THE FRONT LINE

CONTENTS

CHAPTER ONE:

The Part-Time Economy - The Challenge for Leaders   1

- Characteristics of the Part-Time Economy
- Insights and Ideology on How to Best Lead from the Front
- The Challenges the Part-Time Talent Economy Creates for You
- Given the Option, Most People Would Prefer to be Awesome

CHAPTER TWO:

Leading From the Front is an Inside-Out Proposition   21

- The Four Keys to Developing Your Team to Act Like Owners
- The Best Companies Know This Secret
- Does Your Part-Time Talent Have an Impact on Your Customer Experience?
- Customer Loyalty and Brand Loyalty Begin With Employee Loyalty

CHAPTER THREE:

Winning From the Front Line   33

- You Are the Chief Obstacle Remover
- Providing Enablement and Development
- Providing Life Skills That Make Your Part-Time Talent More Marketable
- Rock Star Recognition - Celebrate That of Which You Want to See More
- The Importance of Two Simple Words

CHAPTER FOUR:

Repetition Leads to Excellence   57

- Layered Learning
- Navigating Change
- Repetition Leads to Excellence
- In Order to Affect Behavioral Change, Repetition is Required
- The Importance of Reinforcement and Follow Up

CHAPTER FIVE:

It Does Not Matter What You Say; It is What You Do that Counts!   71

- Culture = Internal Stories
- Brand = External Stories
- Creating Positive Stories is More Important Than Ever!
- What is Your Customer Experience Story?
- Passion is a Positive Contagion
- What Motivates People is What Motivates People
- Productive and Happy? Or, Happy and Productive?
- What is Your Word of Mouth Like?

CHAPTER ONE

The Part-Time Economy - The Challenge for Leaders

■ ■ ■ ■

CHARACTERISTICS OF THE PART-TIME ECONOMY

Today, almost everybody who is entering the workforce is a part-time employee. What I mean by that is your talent may be with you for 20 hours per week, or they may be with you for two years, but almost everybody who enters your organization is not going to make a career out of it.

The new generation entering the workforce views their job opportunities more as gathering a portfolio of experiences as they move through organizations to acquire different skills.

This new part-time economy and part-time workforce presents both unique opportunities and unique challenges for organizations and their leaders.

If you are a leader who wants to be successful, I believe you must learn how to inspire temporary and/or part-time talent.

The challenge for you is how to get the best commitment and desired behavior from your part-time or temporary talent.

However, equally as important as inspiring, developing and getting the best out of your part-time talent is understanding that your team's primary role is to deliver on what your customers value.

I do caution you to be careful not to miss the purpose of developing your part-time talent and full-time team.

The purpose of your workforce, whether it be part time or full time, is to serve your customers in a way that will bring them back.

This is true if you are a front-line supervisor, a middle manager, a regional manager, a Vice President or a CEO.

It is essential that **you** understand the importance of serving and delighting the customers that you and your team come into contact with.

> I believe **the front-line leaders** have the opportunity to see, learn and know more about the customer than any other type of leader in the organization.

If you are leading from the front and observing front-line interactions, then you already know that your customers do not care if the people who are serving them are part-time, full-time, or making a career with you and your organization.

What your customers want is to be served in a way that is fast, friendly and flexible. If you are a smart leader you know that if your customers do not get what they want, they will take their business elsewhere.

The most successful leaders, the type of leaders who are leading from the front, understand an important leadership success secret. The best leaders understand that their primary role is to enable their people to be great, no matter how long they are with the organization.

This means developing your people and removing obstacles for them to serve your customers regardless of whether they have been with you for a day, a month or for their whole career.

It does not matter if an employee is with you for a season, a semester, a month, a year or their entire career. Each and every one of them has the ability to give more energy, more creativity and more passion to you and your business if they choose to. The best leaders learn how to tap into their team's discretionary energy and channel it towards creating exceptional customer experiences.

I have worked with leaders to help them become more effective for the past 30 years in over 70 countries and 15 languages. What I have learned through these experiences is that the world is filled with two types of leaders.

Regardless of the level of the leader, the country of the leader, or the seniority of the leader, what I have experienced is that all leaders fall into two very bifurcated camps.

I define an effective leader as one who develops their team so they give more because they want to, and that discretionary energy is focused on delighting your customers.

Think about your own leadership experiences and be honest with yourself .

Which Leadership Camp do you fall into?

LEADERSHIP CAMP #1:
These leaders assume and operate under the principle that the individuals on their work team would rather be awesome than ordinary.

These leaders have figured out they cannot do everybody's job on their team. Once these leaders have this blinding flash of the obvious, they make the natural conclusion that the only option is to develop and enable each and every individual on their team. These leaders understand their job is to help their team excel with the customer and remove obstacles to excellence.

LEADERSHIP CAMP #2:
**This type of distinct leader has a view point about the individuals on their team, which is,
"How can I protect and prevent these individuals from messing up my career?"**

These leaders often try to do everyone's job, micro-manage and do not develop their team because they assume they will not be with them long anyway.

Unless someone has forced you to get this far in the book, then I assume you are a member of Leadership Camp #1 and desire to capture your team's discretionary energy so you can create awesome experiences with your customers.

> If you only take one thing away from this book, adopt the philosophy of Leadership Camp #1 and put it into practice.
> **This alone will make you a positively-differentiated leader.**

Let's face it. If you get known as the leader who develops their team and creates raving-fan customers, you are likely going to be the one that gets the choice opportunities and promotion, too. But remember, the promotions and accolades that you get need to be treated like the applause you get from developing your part-time and full-time talent and then removing obstacles so they can be awesome.

Before we go any further, let's think about what it would be like to work for a leader in each of the two Leadership Camps. I want you to think about how it would feel from the employee's perspective. I would like you to think about how different the daily work experience is going to be for the individuals who work for the two different Leadership Camps. I would like you to imagine what it would feel like going to work each and every day for an inspired leader from Leadership Camp #1.

When I imagine what it would be like for the individuals working with the leader from Leadership Camp #1, they would likely think something like this; **"My direct supervisor cares about me, knows me beyond the job I do, and is sincerely interested in advancing my skills and development."**

In Camp #2 the leader does not develop his or her people because they think something like this;

"My part-time talent is not going to stay here long anyway, why should I train and develop them?"

Typically, Camp #2 leaders emphasize policies and procedures rather than creating an enabled and flexible workforce.

The individuals in Camp #2 typically would say things like, **"My direct supervisor keeps me in the dark. My leader does not develop my skills and when I ask for help I pretty much get policies and procedures."**

What I have observed in action between these two very different Leadership Camps is that the leaders from Camp #1 have figured out that their talent is their only appreciating asset in their business. **Meaning, they develop their people even if they are temporary or part-time talent.**

The wanna-be leaders who are essentially leadership posers are the ones who do not develop their people and do not remove obstacles to excellence. They fall short because they pretty much assume it is not worth their time because their talent will not stay long anyway.

✻ I asked you earlier in which Leadership Camp you felt you belonged.

I assumed that you most likely felt you belonged in Leadership Camp #1. Because you are reading this book, I also agree that you belong in Leadership Camp #1. However, just because you and I agree, does not mean that's worth a whole lot.

> The more important and critical question for you is: **In what Leadership Camp would your people place you?**

**INSIGHTS AND IDEOLOGY ON
HOW TO BEST LEAD FROM THE FRONT**

Here is a great starting place to ensure you can create the best team with the part-time and full-time talent you have:

Your employee talent requires your direct involvement and support so that they understand what is expected and what is important. It is your primary role to develop your talent and teach them skills that will allow them to excel while they are with you and make them more marketable when they leave you.

Yes, it may seem counter intuitive - but I am pounding the table - urging you to invest in talent that you know is going to depart!

CFOs, CEOs and every other type of executive have challenged my logic over the years, but results over time have proven that my advice is correct - it is undeniably in their best interest to invest in talent that they know will leave. **It is in your best interest too!**

When you develop skills and remove obstacles to excellence, it creates better experiences for the talent that stays with you, and the customers that interact with them.

More importantly, when you establish a reputation for developing skills that make people more marketable, your company will become a magnet for better quality temporary and full-time talent.

In addition to ensuring that you have provided your talent with the learning, development and skills to excel in their roles, your other major responsibility is to remove obstacles that get in their way when serving the customer.

When you lead from the front by providing involvement, support, learning and development, and remove the obstacles that get in the way of your team's excellence, you will be amazed at the results that follow.

> The results that will follow are better internal experiences, enhanced customer experiences, and increased commitment, productivity and **engagement from your team!**

THE CHALLENGES THE PART-TIME TALENT ECONOMY CREATES FOR YOU

If you take a moment to think about it logically, the issue of how to motivate and enable part-time talent is really no different than that of full-time talent. However, most middle managers and front-line associates I speak to tell me the way they are working today is simply not working for them.

When I talk to them, they tell me things like, **"I feel fortunate to have a job, but I'm not really excited to come into work every morning."** I also hear things like, **"I don't feel much appreciation when I'm there, even if I do an excellent job."**

Sadly, one of the universal comments I hear is, **"I don't believe what I am doing really makes a difference."**

When I hear that, I feel empathy for the hard-working folks who toil in an organization that does not call to their higher purpose.

What I also observe and hear from managers all over the globe is that they feel de-energized. They are all running on empty, yet they are answering emails until they fall asleep.

> **THERE IS A MUCH BETTER WAY!**

When leaders focus on enabling their team and removing obstacles to a fast, friendly and hassle-free experience for their customers, this creates energy and alignment. **In turn, a culture of higher productivity can be established within your company.**

What this means to you, Ms. or Mr. Leader, is that you can actually have some balance in your life! The stories and anecdotes that I have just shared about what is not working in most workplaces have an opportunity to be **inverted.**

The POSITIVE iteration of the anecdotes above would read something like this: **"I feel fortunate to be acquiring skills that make me marketable. I'm really excited to come into work every morning."**

"I feel appreciation, especially when I do an awesome job for our customer."

"I find it rewarding to get my most important work accomplished."

This is what happens in a purpose-led, servant leadership organization - one that leverages continual learning, recognition and personalized feedback.

🟩 Your team does the right thing because they want to. Internal service becomes legendary.

🟩 Customers will get a fast, friendly, hassle-free experience every time.

🟩 In the rare occasion when they do not, the recovery process is heroic.

GIVEN THE OPTION, MOST PEOPLE WOULD PREFER TO BE AWESOME

I think when people wake up in the morning and they are preparing to come into your place of business, given the option, they would rather be awesome than average.

You and your organization screen your talent to ensure that you are getting a highly competent and committed new employee. The challenge for you is, once this talent arrives on your team, are you developing and growing them? If the people on your team are not growing, you need to assume the majority of the reason why is you.

There is not a lack of motivation in the workforce today. **There is a lack of development.** Your primary responsibility is to develop more leaders.

I have a hard question for you. If I were to ask your team in private if you, as their coach, leader and direct supervisor, are investing in their development, **what do you think they would say?**

If even one member of your team says, "no," "a little," or "not enough," then you are at an extreme competitive disadvantage.

> **People want to be able to excel.**
> **They want skills that make them more marketable.**

When you provide skills that allow your team to create more authentic, personalized and flexible interactions - not only will they be more engaged, **they will be enabled to solve all your customers' problems, both internally and externally.**

CHAPTER TWO

Leading From the Front Is An Inside-Out Proposition

■ ■ ■ ■

THE FOUR KEYS TO DEVELOPING YOUR TEAM TO ACT LIKE OWNERS

A common wish among the leaders that I speak to, is that their people act more like owners. Meaning, the employees look out for the financial interest of the organization and take care of customers in a way that would make them want to return.

> What are the **four keys** to instilling this type of motivation and engagement?

Before I answer that question, I will tell you that these four keys are not dependent upon the type of organization you are in. These four keys are equally as powerful for any role within the organization.

The following four keys open the door to the discretionary energy of the workforce.

The first key is Share the Truth.

Share the truth about where the organization is going, how it makes and loses money, and how individuals can contribute, get ahead and get the goodies in the organization. If things are not going well in the organization, share the truth about the situation and what the team can do to help.

The second key is Provide Skills.

The purest path to intense engagement is providing skills that make the workforce more marketable and promotable.

The third key is Provide Clarity.

People crave clarity about how they impact the organization, and more importantly, how they can advance in the organization.

The fourth key is Instill Accountability.

The high performers love accountability. Average performers are often uncomfortable with accountability. Low performers try to hide from it.

If you want to motivate and energize your team to act like owners, do not pollute the winner's circle. Providing accountability about how you are going to recognize and reward those who do, from those who do not, is critically important. Regardless if you are a front-line supervisor, or a C-suite executive, these four keys are equally relevant.

> The one **consistent** thing
> regardless of industry,
> regardless of geography
> and regardless of the size of the business,
> is that every world-class organization's
> senior leaders
> **listen to and act on the truth!**

THE BEST COMPANIES KNOW THIS SECRET

Well, actually, it's not a secret; however, the best companies and leaders know, and more importantly, implement this important business process.

> What is the **one common trait** that great companies and leaders share?

Each and every one of the greatest companies and leaders share one common trait - **they all create great internal service cooperation!**

This means creating friendly, authentic and hassle-free experiences from person to person and department to department, at each and every touch point, for each and every teammate and customer.

Each of these great companies and leaders apply the same common sense approach to their success. These great organizations and their great leaders understand that it is impossible to create exceptional customer experiences without great internal service cooperation first!

One of the hallmarks of every legendary customer service organization is that they have awesome internal service cooperation.

As I continually reinforce, I believe a leader's number one job is to enable their people with skills so they can create differentiated customer experiences. The second most important job for a leader is to remove stupid policies, procedures and obstacles that get in the way of internal and external service excellence.

The best service organizations, the best leaders, are those who are seen as fast, responsive and easy to do business with. As I have said, I have never seen this happen without the one common trait: **exceptional internal service cooperation!** This internal service cooperation enables the organization and the leader's team to be more flexible and more responsive in anticipating and serving the needs of their customers.

How To Enhance Your Team'...

1. Stay Positive. Maintain the same positive attitude with your internal partners as you would with an external customer.

2. Honor Commitments. When you make a commitment to a co-worker, keep it.

3. Step Out of Your "Silo." Network with co-workers from other areas of the organization to understand the internal service workflow.

4. Negotiate Expecta... Share how another int... service provider can b... assist you in serving an external cus...

If you want to be a leader who is seen as creating great internal service cooperation, then I encourage you to use the following ideas to enhance your team's internal service cooperation:

■ **Stay Positive.** Maintain the same positive, upbeat attitude with your internal partners and customers as you would with external customers.

■ **Honor Commitments.** When you make a commitment to a co-worker, keep it.

■ **Communicate Often.** The best customer service is created from high-touch, high-tech communication environments.

■ **Negotiate Expectations.** Discover how your output can be a better input for a work colleague. Share how another internal service provider can better assist you in serving an external customer.

Internal Service Cooperation:

Be Polite.
Treat co-workers with the same courtesy as you would a customer.

Communicate Often.
The best customer service is created from a high-touch, high-tech communication environment.

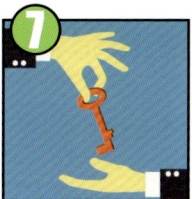
Be Helpful.
Look for ways to directly or indirectly support a customer or co-worker.

Stay Positive.
Starting positive and staying positive are the most important elements to creating personalized service interactions.

■ **Step Out of Your "Silo."** Network with co-workers from other areas of the organization to understand the internal service workflow.

■ **Be Polite.** Treat co-workers with the same courtesy as you would customers, and help them be responsive and efficient to your external customers.

■ **Be Helpful.** Look for ways to directly or indirectly support a customer or co-worker.

■ **Stay Positive.** Yes, it is so important I felt I had to say it twice.

> **Starting positive and staying positive** are the most important elements to creating memorable service experiences.

When you align your internal service delivery to be better, faster and different than your competition, it will help create exceptional customer experiences.

Remember, your external service cannot possibly be better than your internal service.

DOES YOUR PART-TIME TALENT HAVE AN IMPACT ON YOUR CUSTOMER EXPERIENCE?

I have been working with senior leaders since the early 1980s on strategies and learning that help create exceptional employee and customer experiences. One of the first things I typically ask senior leadership is if there is anyone inside of their organization they think **does not** have an impact on the external customer's experience. In the history of asking this question, not one senior leader has ever identified someone in their organization that did not impact their external customer experience, loyalty and perception of the brand.

It does not matter if this individual is with you for a day, a week, a season, a semester or their entire career. You need to understand that every person inside your organization can - and does - impact the customer experience, and thus, customer loyalty. Creating customer loyalty requires that you first have great internal service from individual to individual and work group to work group, so you can consistently create exceptional experiences for your external customers.

Leading from the front and developing temporary talent requires focusing on internal service cooperation. This internal service cooperation, in my mind, is one of the biggest advantages you can create as a leader. Having an engaged and enabled workforce that is aligned around the internal brand enables you to be more flexible, responsive and memorable in servicing the needs and expectations of your external customers.

CUSTOMER LOYALTY AND BRAND LOYALTY BEGIN WITH EMPLOYEE LOYALTY

If you want to be known as someone who is leading from the front, then I challenge you to look for ways to align your internal service delivery so that it is better, faster and different than your competition.

If you are an individual contributor, I challenge you to share ideas with whomever internally provides you input for your work. These ideas should cover how their input can help you do your job better, faster or more memorably.

Remember, your customers call you for help and answers. It takes great internal service cooperation to provide seamless, flexible, hassle-free service.

> **This is what each and every one of your customers want!**

CHAPTER THREE

Winning From the Front Line

■ ■ ■ ■

**YOU ARE THE
CHIEF OBSTACLE REMOVER**

There are all sorts of different definitions and descriptions out there for leaders, leadership, management and influence. If you think about it, it does not matter what level leader or manager you are, or whether you are leading a local charitable organization or a Fortune 50 global company.

As I have stressed, leading from the front requires focusing on two primary roles:

- Developing other leaders by enabling your team.
- Removing obstacles that get in the way of excellence.

If you want to become known as the Chief Obstacle Remover, then I suggest that you focus on removing all obstacles in these three arenas:

- Internal service cooperation.
- Sales and service touch points.
- Anything that gets in the way of an exceptional experience for your customers.

If you become known as a Chief Obstacle Remover I guarantee you will become more promotable yourself.

Time and time again, I have seen leaders who focus on becoming the Chief Obstacle Remover achieve significantly better results than their peers. The type of results that are sustainable.

The combination of developing your people with skills, and then becoming a Chief Obstacle Remover is analogous to taking the parking brake off when you are driving a car. By removing obstacles (releasing the parking brake), you are creating a surge of energy for your team, your department, your store, your property, your group, your division and your organization.

The most awesome result of becoming a Chief Obstacle Remover is that as you continue to to remove obstacles to excellence, the positive momentum not only continues, but typically accelerates.

Here are three principles to assist you in achieving world-class status:

Address and remove any and all obstacles in your internal service cooperation.

Eliminate any obstacles in your sales, service or delivery touch points.

Remove any obstacles that get in the way of exceptional experiences with your customers. Everything else is just white noise.
Focus on your people, focus on what your customers value and focus on improving the experience.

If you want to be the type of leader that creates intense levels of engagement and exceptional customer experiences then get out of your office and practice managing by walking around.

Managing by walking around means experiencing your experience. This means viewing things both from your customer's perspective and most importantly, your team's perspective.

You should not wait for your company to be featured in an episode of Undercover Boss to understand what the experiences are like for your front-line associates. In fact, it is my belief and experience that your front-line associates can tell you more about what needs to be changed, added or deleted from the organizational experience than anybody else in your organization. It doesn't matter if they have been with you for one month, three months or 36 months, they have a story to tell and you should be listening to it.

Your talent, whether temporary or full time, should be excited about your mission, vision and values, but if they are not enabled to do the job, that excitement will lead to frustration rather than exceptional experiences.

How do you respond when there is an obstacle to your talents' performance?

In addition to being engaged and enabled, employees need a work environment where they can create positive experiences and have an impact on the customer service process.

Are you providing this type of work environment?

Part-time and full-time talent who are not just engaged, but also energized and enabled, produce far greater financial benefits than employees who are simply engaged. Employee engagement is about sustaining and enhancing the organizational culture.

Your culture is nothing more than the cumulative effect of stories being shared internally by your employees.

> If you want to change your culture,
> you have to change your stories.
> To change your stories,
> **you have to change your
> employee experiences.**

> **Engaged Employees:**
>
> Create memorable service experiences for customers.
>
> •
>
> Help each other to do their jobs more efficiently.
>
> •
>
> Stay 15 minutes late to help a customer with a question.
>
> •
>
> Refuse to spread or partake in negative gossip.
>
> •
>
> Refer to the organization as a great place to work.

When your organization creates the internal conditions that enable people to excel at their jobs and serve customers exceptionally, this will drive high levels of employee engagement while simultaneously energizing the employees.

It does not get much better than that, does it?

PROVIDING ENABLEMENT AND DEVELOPMENT

Just think about the best leader, manager or boss you have ever had. I bet if you think about his or her qualities you will find that the best leader you ever had developed you and enabled you by providing learning that made you more marketable, but most importantly he or she removed obstacles to your performance.

As I travel the world to work with some of the biggest brands, I am always amazed at the incredible results that the obstacle removers in those companies create compared to those who lead by command and control.

Personally, my best boss was Dr. Marjorie Blanchard who co-founded The Ken Blanchard Companies. Marjorie was the type of leader who liked to surround herself with an eclectic group of thinkers. She was one to always expose me to tremendous development and learning opportunities while also permitting me to re-write the rules. She supported me by removing obstacles including silly policies and outdated procedures that had outlived their useful date.

She even enabled me to create a separate division and company that offered performance improvement work embedded in our clients, implementing the Blanchard philosophy.

Those experiences and her leadership changed my life for the better, forever. I will bet your best boss impacted you in a similar fashion.

So, what type of leader does your team say you are?

Are you leading in a way that gives you the opportunity to be perceived as I perceived Marjorie? Or, are your leadership characteristics more similar to a Leadership Camp #2?

There have been millions upon millions of dollars spent around the globe on employee engagement efforts and initiatives. As most Human Resources (HR) and Organizational Development (OD) professionals know, the global statistics around employee engagement are still quite poor. Despite all the time, effort and energy expended, it seems to me organizations are missing one of the key ingredients.

In my experience, the missing ingredient in many organizations around the world is enablement. Enablement means providing your employees with the skills needed to excel today and the development needed to advance tomorrow.

> **When you deliver skills that increase the competency of your workers, they always become more energized and engaged!**

How do you ensure you deliver this important missing ingredient? (If it were easy, everyone would be doing it.)

To create an organizational culture that can sustain and enhance employee engagement, the organization and the HR and OD professionals need to spend ten times the amount of time, energy and resources following up and reinforcing learning and engagement principles as they do designing and delivering them.

Unfortunately, as I travel the world, I see most organizations spending ten times the amount of time, energy and resources designing and delivering the learning and engagement principles and almost zero time following up and reinforcing them.

Remember, good intentions not delivered equals squat.

> The only way to deliver the missing ingredient to your employee engagement strategy is to **create enablement** through learning, follow up and reinforcement.

I have been engaged in some emotionally-charged debates in HR and OD communities regarding the importance of enablement and energy as it relates to employee engagement. I am all for engagement; however, I view it as an outcome of enabling your

your associates and removing obstacles so that you can foster their passion and energy. When you do that, engagement flows naturally.

Today, decisions are made at every level of your organization. The seemingly "low level" decisions are extremely important in today's fast-paced organizations.

If you think about it, front-line workers should know more about their areas of specialization than anybody else, so their decisions are likely to have an impact throughout the company.

Peter Drucker stressed that every organization needs performance in these three major areas:

Direct results.

Building your values and reaffirming them.

Developing and enabling people for tomorrow.

> **Ask yourself this:**
> Are you enabling your people and fostering their passion?
> Or, are you trying to make them happy by trying to engage them?

Here are seven steps to create better engagement and enablement with your work team:

ONE

Provide engaging learning to develop skills that make your employees more marketable, ideally internally, but maybe someday externally.

TWO

Ensure there is proper differentiation in how you rate performance amongst your employees. There is nothing worse than polluting the winner's circle with low performers.

THREE

Remove obstacles and bad or outdated business practices or policies that can negatively affect employee enablement.

FOUR

Leverage your employees' distinct abilities and ensure the right people are in the right role.

FIVE

Take a look at your leaders and your own competencies and management style and make sure they are aligned to motivate and enable your team.

SIX

Focus on non-monetary rewards such as career growth and recognition programs.

SEVEN

Ensure you have created and communicated a clear link between performance and rewards within your work group and organization.

> Remember,
> I define engagement as:
> **Doing the right thing,
> at the right time,
> the right way,
> for the right reasons.**

If your talent is engaged, enabled and energized, then they will be in a position to consistently do the right thing, the right way, at the right time, to create exceptional experiences from the inside out.

PROVIDING LIFE SKILLS THAT MAKE YOUR PART-TIME TALENT MORE MARKETABLE

People are not a liability. They are one of the few business assets that can appreciate significantly over time. This appreciation does not happen by accident. This appreciation of human capital, this increase of productivity and profit comes from skills.

However, skills alone are not enough.

Your job as a leader is to remove the stuff that gets in the way of excellence.

Excellence internally.

Excellence externally.

Excellence now.

Excellence always.

Excellence at every touch point.

Excellence with every interaction.

When you do that as a leader, all of your people will be as valuable as a rare gem.

One of the key differences between an organizational development professional and a weenie is that the best organizational development professionals, learning officers and trainers know that to create enablement requires layering in skills over time with a focus on follow up, reinforcement and action planning.

These learning officers and organizational development pros know that when they create enablement through layering in skills it releases energy in their workforce. As a result of this enhanced enablement and energy, the natural outcome is increased employee engagement.

Creating employee engagement without a culture of learning is like planting a seed in cement and hoping it will grow.

> **The key to
> intense employee engagement**
> is to create a culture
> where leaders are held accountable
> for developing others.

When organizational leaders focus on providing meaningful work, the right skills and development, employee engagement always improves.

It is only logical, don't you agree?

ROCK STAR RECOGNITION - CELEBRATE THAT OF WHICH YOU WANT TO SEE MORE

Do you feel it is important to celebrate service excellence?

When I ask this question in person, whether in a board room or talking with a front-line associate, I almost always get the same answer:

"Of course I think celebrating service excellence is important."

I feel talking with a front-line associate is the most visceral way to learn about an organization and its sales and service interactions. When I do this, I will always follow up by asking, "Do you get recognition and/or rewards?"

Almost universally, the answer is, "Very little," or "Not at all."

In my mind, this is absolutely crazy! With companies spending millions and millions of dollars trying to improve their customer loyalty, why would they not recognize, reward and celebrate - creating a fun, friendly, authentic interaction?

When I am talking to senior executives, almost 100% of the time they agree it is good business sense and important to celebrate service excellence.

**Now why don't you go ahead
and answer the same two questions?**

■ How important do you feel it is to celebrate service excellence?

■ When was the last time you recognized service excellence, whether it be internal or external?

THE IMPORTANCE OF TWO SIMPLE WORDS

How does two words plus five words equal millions?

It is definitely true, both in my experience as an individual contributor, but even more so in my role providing coaching and guidance to global corporations, that "thank you" are potentially the most powerful two words to show appreciation.

When you say "thank you" it does not mean simply appreciating your associates.

This means saying **"Thank You."**
To your boss.
To your parents.
To your peers.
To your spouse.
To your colleagues and co-workers.
To your friends and extended family.
To your children and to your children's friends.

Yes, this means saying "Thank You" to your

direct reports and associates in other departments.

Showing appreciation and saying "Thank You" is tremendously important and tremendously powerful.

Even more powerful than saying "Thank You" is combining this appreciation with one or more of the five word questions below.

Before I give you this powerful recipe to create millions of dollars worth of positive impact - I must caution you:

Do not ever ask these five word questions unless you intend to act on them!

> If, however, you are committed
> to using **"Thank You"**
> with one or more
> of these powerful
> five word questions and actions,
> then you are on your way
> to creating
> **intense levels of enablement!**

When you appreciate upward, downward, diagonally and horizontally, in combination with the following five-word questions and actions, I guarantee you will create enablement and engagement. You will unleash intense levels of positive energy into your organization and relationships.

The Power Five on Five

How can I enable you?

What skills do you desire?

What obstacles obstruct your excellence?

What help do you need?

What is your desired recognition?

> **The old work contract is over!**

Part-time and full-time talent is not going to trade job security for loyalty.

Your employees want skills; skills that will make

them more marketable.

Not some time in the future.

They want skills that will make them more marketable NOW.

They want skills that will help them excel with customers. They want skills that will make them promotable at your company, or yes, some place else some day.

CHAPTER FOUR

Repetition Leads to Excellence

■ ■ ■ ■

LAYERED LEARNING

What do the most admired global companies all have in common?

I have traveled almost four million miles working with organizations and their leaders, helping them create cultures that produce exceptional employee and customer experiences. The one thing each and every one of these most-admired companies shares in common is they provide skills that make their associates more marketable.

Each and every one of the most admired global companies provides "life skills" to their workforce.

These corporations know that the best type of learning requires repetition and reinforcement versus fire-hose doses of information.

Here are the mistakes that the unadmired and ineffective corporations make when delivering

learning to their associates.

The unadmired try to give learners as much information as they can, as fast as they can. I describe this as being analogous to drinking through a fire hose.

The unadmired do a poor job of converting their instructor-led content to an eLearning environment.

Unless it is mandatory, almost no one will watch a boring eLearning module with a talking head for 40, 50, 60 minutes or more - especially if this content is subtitled or voiced over. It is not because the content isn't good or helpful, it is because it is delivered in a way that is guaranteed to NOT produce a sustainable change or result.

The biggest mistake is that too much time,

energy and effort is spent on designing and delivering the learning and too little time spent on following up, reinforcing and implementing the learning. Repetition is the mother of all learning and life force for all positive change!

So what is the best way to deliver learning?

One bite at a time!

Here's an analogy. The best way to eat an elephant is one bite at a time. Although I don't know that anyone would actually want to eat an elephant, I do know this is an analogy for the best way to tackle a big task, project or goal - to break it into smaller pieces and accomplish it over time.

If we want to continue with analogies - I think most corporate learning is similar to watching a python swallow a pig. Yes, they can get it down, but it is way too much, way too fast.

The right way to eat an elephant is also the right way to create massive and sustainable learning and cultural change - in small chunks layered in over time, with reinforcement and contextualization in between each bite.

NAVIGATING CHANGE

Most individuals, teams and organizations often times fear and/or resist change. If you think about it, change requires doing something different. Changing for the better requires learning and applying something new.

Even the rare organizations who are open and willing to change often make the most common mistake of doing too much too fast.

The best learning, the best change, the kind that is sustainable, is done in bite-sized chunks with the proper amount of support and reinforcement in between.

> The reality is,
> if you are not changing,
> **you are not growing.**

If you are not getting better, you are not just staying the same, you are falling behind.

Significant change happens as a result of the cumulative effect of small incremental improvements.

Change requires practice. If you want to create change, whether personally or professionally, it requires repetition and practice. I have said it before and I will say it again and again: Repetition is truly the mother of all learning and the life force for positive change.

Trying something new will create discomfort. If you are comfortable, you are likely not trying anything new.

Furthermore, if you're trying something new you won't get it perfect the first time.

That is why repetition and practice can help create more precision, more productivity and more profit.

If you want to create change, you have to get through the discomfort of layering in a new skill or behavior.

However, once that new skill or behavior becomes part of your repertoire you no longer feel uncomfortable, and that might be a good time to think about layering in another new skill!

> Repetition
> is the Mother of All Learning.
>
> **Repetition
> is the Mother of All Learning.**

REPETITION
LEADS TO EXCELLENCE

> "Practice Does Not Make Perfect.
> **Perfect Practice Makes Perfect!"**
>
> - Vince Lombardi

The quote above from Vince Lombardi is an important one. If you do something repetitively wrong, you ingrain that poor behavior in your daily routine.

However, if you leverage repetition and follow a proven process then that repetition produces universally positive results!

IN ORDER TO AFFECT BEHAVIORAL CHANGE, REPETITION IS REQUIRED

Why do you think advertising agencies believe in repetition? The science is undeniable. One of the challenges with trying to make cultural change, behavior change or learning transfer in organizations is the fact that change means you are doing something new.

Because change requires new behaviors, and new behaviors create discomfort, most people want to go back to the way things were. To get over the feeling of discomfort associated with change, it is important to use repetition and reinforcement when introducing new skills and behaviors into the work place.

> **It is completely unrealistic
> to expect a learner to get it right
> each and every time.
> However,
> with repetition and perfect practice,
> excellence will result!**

Billions upon billions of dollars are wasted in organizations all over the world every year because of the lack of reinforcement and repetition of learning. If workers can't retain the knowledge or competency, then it is worthless to their colleagues and customers. The key to retention and the more critical step of retrieval is layering skills and competencies in bite-sized doses.

THE IMPORTANCE OF REINFORCEMENT AND FOLLOW UP

If you cannot retrieve the knowledge, it is worthless.

Companies of all sizes around the world spend tens of billions of dollars per year on corporate education, learning and development. Many Chief Learning Officers and Learning and Development professionals have an intense focus on competency and skill retention. Being able to retain a skill or competency is important in learning transfer; however, more important, is the ability to retrieve that content or competency when you need it to make a difference with a customer or a colleague.

What I'm talking about is analogous to a filing system.

Picture a dentist who has his or her office manager filing patient records, which in learning is equivalent to retention. Corporations are often measured on retention and/or recall after a learning event.

In this case, if the dentist asked, "How many of the patient records have you retained?" The office manager replies, "100%." Then, when the next patient arrives and the dentist says, "Mary, can you please pull Mrs. Anderson's file?" Mary looks at the dentist and says, "I'm not sure where it is. I can not seem to find it."

Poor Mary can't access the file when she needs it.

This is what so often happens in corporate learning and education. We spend so much time designing and measuring the delivery and retention of the content and almost no time following up the ability of the learner to retrieve the skills, content and/or competency when they need it!

The key to retrieving skills and competencies, the key to learning ROI is repetition and reinforcement.

> Remember,
> transferring a skill or competency from
> a learning environment to the work environment
> is best done in **bite-size chunks!**

When I speak to leaders I often talk about the "leaving learning optional syndrome." When organizations and their employees view learning and development as an event versus an ongoing process, often times the employees believe that "this too shall pass."

Just imagine an employee taking a manhole cover, placing it over his or her head and hiding out until the program of the month, quarter or year passes by.

However, when an organization invests in its human capital, it is critically important that ten times the amount of time, energy and resources is spent following up and reinforcing learning and development as is spent designing and delivering it.

> **When organizations and their employees have follow up, reinforcement, accountability and repetition,**
> **the ROI is always significant.**

To realize the full benefits of employee engagement, you and your organization need the enablement and experience factor.

Your organization's employees can be excited about your mission, vision and values, but if they are not enabled to do the job, that excitement will lead to frustration rather than exceptional experiences.

In addition to being engaged and enabled, employees need to work in an environment where they can create positive experiences and have an impact on the service experience improvement process. Employees who are not just engaged, but also energized and enabled, produce far greater financial benefits than employees who are simply engaged.

CHAPTER FIVE

It Does Not Matter What You Say; It is What You Do that Counts!

CULTURE =
INTERNAL STORIES

Now, more than ever, our employees and customers know the difference between exceptional experiences and those that are not. And today, these experiences and stories can be shared quickly and widely with the internet and social media. The best organizations with legendary service create exceptional experiences for their employees, who in turn, create exceptional experiences for their customers. Let's hope your experiences are exceptional.

Remember, your culture and your brand are nothing more than the cumulative effect of the stories being told about you. Experiences lead to stories. The cumulative effect of those stories will either make or break you. Do not make the mistake of thinking people will not notice and share the experiences they are having internally and externally.

BRAND =
EXTERNAL STORIES

Many millions of dollars are spent on a company's internal communication and branding strategy. That money could be better spent developing and engaging employees.

At the end of the day who are you more likely to believe, Madison Avenue or a front-line employee? Do you believe what you read in a magazine, hear in a TV ad, or see in an online ad? Or do you believe a personal experience story from somebody you know?

Companies spend zillions of dollars on communications and branding, but at the end of the day brand is nothing more than the cumulative stories the customer and stakeholders share.

Your culture is nothing more than the stories employees share.

Seems to me that if companies spent less time

on "branding" and more time on developing competencies, sharing business strategies, and supporting and involving front-line associates, the increased levels of engagement would take care of the culture and the brand. Don't get me wrong, communications plays a vital role in maintaining brand integrity and is smart for any business. But intense focus on communications often overshadows the simple answer that lies right inside the company walls - brand and culture are created from the inside out.

Teaching, enabling and removing obstacles, in my opinion, plays a more vital role in creating a brand and culture than communications.

I am glad that I wake up every day with a focus on these issues.

CREATING POSITIVE STORIES IS MORE IMPORTANT THAN EVER!

I believe that in today's personalization economy, people crave authentic and hassle-free interactions. As a result of the explosion of social media, stories have a more powerful ripple effect than ever in history. Service and the perceptions around the experiences are unique because they are engineered, produced, consumed and evaluated simultaneously.

In every interaction there are only three potential outcomes:

A negative story.
How was Joe's?
"Joe's diner is so bad you should eat anywhere BUT there!"

No story.
How was Joe's?
"Meh, no better or no worse than the competition."

A positive story.

How was Joe's?

"Oh my gosh! That place was unbelievable.
The milkshakes had real ice cream!
I felt like I was going back in time.
What a great experience!"

It is obvious that two out of the three possible outcomes are negative and the third story is what we are all after - customers who refer others!

Stories today can have a dramatic affect on everything from a product, a brand, a company, a politician and even governments and their leaders. It is important to remember that if you want to change your stories, you first have to change the experiences.

> **If you want to create experiences
> that are positively better,
> those interactions and experiences better be
> authentic, fast, fun and hassle free.**

WHAT IS YOUR CUSTOMER EXPERIENCE STORY?

Your "customer experience story" is literally how your customers perceive their interactions with your company. Those interactions occur at each step along a customer journey. That journey begins when people realize that you offer a product or service they might want, then compare your offer to other options. If things go your way, they will buy from you. Then they will use what they bought or experience your service. If they encounter a problem, they will call for support.

At every touch point with your organization, your customers judge the experiences!

Think about your organization and think about your organization's purpose and brand promise. Then, think about the employees in your organization and if their behaviors and actions are aligned with your brand and brand promise.

Engaged employees who successfully represent the brand provide a significant and unique competitive advantage. Creating brand ambassadors versus disengaged employees is one of the most important elements of creating customer loyalty.

Companies that foster brand ambassadors versus companies that mismanage disengaged employees create radically different results.

It is imminently logical that your external brand and the stories about it can never be better or stronger than your internal employee brand and stories. After thinking about your brand and your organization's employee actions and alignment, what do you have? Ambassadors or mismanaged, disengaged employees?

If you do not know the answer or are unsure, I will give you a hint; try shopping your organization.

That will give you a clear answer.

PASSION IS A POSITIVE CONTAGION

While most contagions are bad, wouldn't it be awesome if a contagion of positivity spread through your organization like wild fire?

In service as well as in life, it is always much more fulfilling to have an interaction with someone who is competent, committed, authentic and friendly. In fact, these are just the type of interactions that employees will stay for and customers will pay for. In other words, it makes for a more pleasurable environment in which to work and do business.

Positive Stories Start From the Inside!

Stories are the most powerful and viral marketing method available to you. Statistics say that 68 percent of your customers are likely to leave you over a negative service experience. A common mistake I see organizations all over the world making in their attempts to improve their positive stories, is that they start from the outside in. I have been fortunate enough to work with some of the leading organizations that understand the pitfalls of this approach.

> Universally,
> the one thing I have found is that
> **differentiated experiences
> and positive stories
> start from the inside.**

The best organizations, the ones that you and I like to do business with, and often pay a premium for the opportunity to do so, are the ones that deliver fast, friendly, hassle-free service.

If you work backwards from the experiences that we all pay for, you will see they all emanate from **great internal service cooperation.**

WHAT MOTIVATES PEOPLE IS WHAT MOTIVATES PEOPLE

A critical business secret I have learned is, "What motivates people *is* what motivates people!"

Yes, it is a blinding flash of the obvious! **What motivates people *is* what motivates people!**

It is critically important as a front line leader, and truly important for all leaders, to leverage recognition, feedback and praise.

But, a word of caution: too often organizations make the mistake of trying to create a program, or a one size fits all approach, when it comes to providing recognition, feedback and praise.

This simply does not work.

When you enable employees with skills and you remove obstacles so that they can be awesome, it is vital to provide recognition, feedback and praise, so that those employees continue to repeat their awesome performances.

The best recognition is situational.

> **That is one size fits one.**

You need to tailor and personalize your praise, feedback and recognition so it is motivational for the person who receives it.

This requires getting to know the different triggers for your talent.

Remember, often times the best recognition and feedback is a simple "thank you" or personal praising, which can be immensely meaningful and can be a key to sustaining a high performance culture.

> **What motivates you is different than what motivates me.**

As a leader it is important that you leverage situational recognition as a tool in your toolbox to keep your part-time and full-time talent engaged, focused and energized. Recognition is about helping people become more productive.

PRODUCTIVE AND HAPPY?
OR, HAPPY AND PRODUCTIVE?

I have had my share of debates with senior leaders and even more than my fair share with HR professionals on this very question.

The key is not to run around trying to make your people feel happy. If that were the case we could simply send all of our people to Disneyland and let them spend every day there, as we know that it is the happiest place on earth!

We all know that is absurd, and yet these same HR professionals and senior leaders spend millions of dollars on surveys and assessments to get a pulse or a baseline of employee engagement and the issues that are preventing them from being "fully engaged."

I think we have over-baked the turkey when it comes to assessing engagement and trying to ensure they have "a best friend at work" today.

What I personally see and experience in

organizations both large and small on this continent and all over the world is that engagement and sustainable results are created not by making people happy, but by enabling them.

By enabling I mean ensuring that they have the skills, competencies and career path to excel with customers, to produce outstanding results, and to know if they do those things, they will be rewarded, recognized and promoted.

> **Start on the inside.**
>
> When your organization creates the internal conditions
> that enable people to excel at their jobs
> **and serve customers exceptionally,**
> it will drive high levels
> of employee engagement
> **while simultaneously energizing employees.**

60 - Second Organizational Employee Survey

☐ Are you getting the **skills** that allow you to excel in serving an internal or external customer?

☐ Does your direct supervisor **actively remove obstacles or procedures** that get in your way of serving an internal or external customer?

☐ Do you feel when you produce valued results **you are recognized and rewarded?**

☐ Do you feel people are promoted based on **competence** and **results** produced?

> How do
> your employees rate
> **you?**

Regardless if you are a senior leader or an HR professional, if you try to make your people feel "happy" **you are caught in the B.S. trap** - the "Behavioral Sciences" trap.

Now, if you are an individual contributor you may find yourself in an organization that is stuck in the B.S. trap: assessing, monitoring, doing pulse surveys, but not providing the type of learning that makes you more marketable or actively removing obstacles that get in your way of serving an internal or external customer.

So, if you read that last paragraph and said, "That sounds just like my organization" then I have a secret that will help you be more productive, more marketable and yes, more happy.

For those individuals in organizations that are stuck in the B.S. trap, here is your life preserver - and a way to rise out of the pack.

The key is for you to realize: **You have to be there anyway - so why not be magnificent?**

If you choose to look at every interaction as an opportunity to create delight, and you live those actions daily, you will be blown away at how productive and happy you will become.

Exactly in that order.

Productive first, happy second.

People Who Excel Feel Good About Themselves.

WHAT IS YOUR WORD OF MOUTH LIKE?

In my experience, an individual's stories are pretty much the same in all aspects of their life.

>What do your customers say about you?
>What do your teammates say about you?
>What do your friends say about you?
>What does your family say about you?
>What does your dog bark about you?

If you delight your customers, you likely have a habit of delighting **everyone** with whom you interact.

And I bet if you don't, you pretty much irritate everyone in your ecosystem.

> **So, what is your word of mouth like?**
> If you want it to be great, you better create fast, friendly, authentic interactions with everyone you come into contact with.

If You've Made it This Far - You are Already a Winner!

What I mean by this is if you haven't skipped to the end of the book first, then you possess the extraordinary quality of persistence, follow up and a commitment to learning. That is something that is highly contagious and infectious in the most positive of ways.

The biggest organizational sport in the world is still "boss watching." I don't care what level of leader you are or what level of leader you aspire to be, you must understand that organizational members look upwards for direction, support, vision and guidance. Or said differently, people look up the hierarchy to figure out what is important, what gets reinforced, what gets tolerated and what gets recognized and rewarded.

As I mentioned earlier, both you and your people have to be there anyway, **so why not choose to be awesome?**

As I have stressed, a great reputation to earn

is one of creating positive word of mouth for providing life skills.

> **These are the types of skills that make your talent more marketable, more promotable and more exceptional.**

The only way that is going to happen is if you go first.

Apply the principles in this book that make sense to you and leave the rest behind.

I challenge you to commit to and follow up each and every day with the ideas and principles that work for you.

When you do this, the outcome of your personal "boss watching" will create a positive contagion with your teammates and your place of business.

When you take the lead and do it consistently, others will naturally follow.

> That is what
> **Leading From the Front Line**
> is truly all about!

CSIinternational

www.CSIperformance.com • 855.231.8407

Additional Services Offered:

Through our customer-intimate relationships, CSI International delivers global learning and performance solutions that create exceptional employee and customer experiences for our client companies. The result of us helping you create these exceptional experiences is that your customers will stay longer, buy more and tell others.

MORE ABOUT CSI INTERNATIONAL'S SOLUTIONS:

Global Learning:

Your personalized Layered Learning℠ program delivers only the necessary content and competencies to your employees at exactly the right time and in bite-sized doses, with a focus on action planning, reinforcement and accountability. CSI International delivers its global learning solutions seamlessly across all devices, including mobile.

Global Employee Performance:

Your global performance platform helps you recognize and reward your employees for exceptional achievements, enabling and motivating them to maintain success. CSI International's global performance solutions offer a broad selection of rewards that are culturally relevant and sourced in country.

Upcoming books by the author:

Personalization Principles for the Winners of the Personalization Economy

Leading from the Front Line Field Guide with ATD

ACKNOWLEDGEMENTS

My first business mentor, Dr. Ken Blanchard, taught me an important life-long lesson. That is, the power of praise and a personalized thank you.

I would like to thank and praise Marjorie and Ken Blanchard for starting me on my organizational development journey.

A special thanks to Rachel Russotto, Connie Grant and Jennifer Budinsky for their tireless, dedicated, insightful and creative editing of this book. Most importantly, they deserve a praising for their flexibility and for putting their creative hearts into this book.

A praising is also appropriate for Patsy Psichogios, yes, we are related! My sister has provided awesome graphics and design since the '90's for my various business ventures. The cover art and page design are another example of her awesome creativity.

"Mahalo" to Tanner J. and Mary P. for proofreading.

I would like to praise each and every one of my colleagues at CSI International who work every day on behalf of our clients endeavoring to make these principles come to life. Especially Ashley Tolfa and Dan Rogers who have created exceptional experiences in extraordinary circumstances.

A special praising to Matt Lordly who is the snowboarding, skateboarding, sailing, globe-trotting alchemist whose elegant code drives CSI International's mobile, global layered learning.

A special thank you to my partner Steven Brown who has believed in the vision before others understood it, and to his beautiful bride Kimberlee who has become a dear friend.

I would also like to thank Mark Peterman for connecting me with Ron Lippock at The Association for Talent Development where the initial idea for this book was germinated.

A praising for Ron Lippock's flexibility in allowing me to write a more in depth Leading From the Front Line field guide for the Association of Talent Development to be released in early 2016.

The most important praising goes to my parents Tom and Mary, who supported my uniqueness and continue to do so today.